At David C Cook, we equip the local church around the corner and around the globe to make disciples. Come see how we are working together—go to **www.davidccook.com**. Thank you!

David C Cook
transforming lives together

PARTICIPANT'S GUIDE

Wait and See

PARTICIPANT'S GUIDE

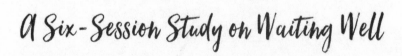

A Six-Session Study on Waiting Well

Wendy Pope

David C Cook

transforming lives together

WAIT AND SEE PARTICIPANT'S GUIDE
Published by David C Cook
4050 Lee Vance Drive
Colorado Springs, CO 80918 U.S.A.

David C Cook U.K., Kingsway Communications
Eastbourne, East Sussex BN23 6NT, England

The graphic circle C logo is a registered trademark of David C Cook.

LCCN 2017936998
ISBN 978-1-4347-1209-7
eISBN 978-0-8307-7278-0

The Team: Matt Lockhart, Tim Peterson, Laura Derico,
Nick Lee, Jack Campbell, Susan Murdock
Cover Design: Amy Konyndyk
Cover Photo: Getty Images

Printed in the United States of America
First Edition 2017

1 2 3 4 5 6 7 8 9 10

081717

Contents

Welcome

Welcome to the *Wait and See Participant's Guide.* I'm thrilled to be doing Bible study with you! And I'm so thankful that we get to work things out together and learn about this subject that has become such a passion and need of mine over many years—waiting well. (I even wrote a whole book about it—*Wait and See: Finding Peace in God's Pauses and Plans.*)

This Bible study is unlike any you've ever done. I kept you in mind throughout the entire creative process. You, the woman who wants so badly to study God's Word but doesn't know where or how to start. You, the woman who gets so excited to start a new Bible study but stops going to class because you didn't get your blanks filled in. You, the woman who loves to study the Bible but doesn't want to study alone.

This study is for you! Come with me to a Bible study without guilt and homework—the Bible study you've been waiting for!

For six sessions you will join your friends—some you know, and others you may meet during your group time—to study God's Word. Each class will begin with a ten-minute video teaching segment followed by a teacher-led discussion. Then the real fun begins! You and your friends answer the study questions—together. Friends don't let friends leave empty blanks in their Bible study. And all God's girls said, *"Amen!"*

The days of condemnation for incomplete homework pages and sitting out of Bible study because of it are over … in Jesus's name. Liberty in Bible study begins here. It begins today!

And if you like to have a little something to do during the week, I haven't forgotten you. At the end of each lesson is a section called "On Your Own … If You Want To." This small assignment is not mandatory, nor is it a prerequisite for admission to the next session. No one will even ask whether you completed it. What a relief, right?

I've tucked a prayer deep in my heart for you. This prayer aligns beautifully with Jesus's words in John 8:32, "Then you will know the truth, and the truth will set you free." The Greek word for "know" in this verse is *ginóskō*, meaning "to know through personal experience."

I pray you experience God so intimately and personally that you don't wait for the next Bible study to continue your learning. I pray this study ignites a passion in your heart to study on your own. I pray you will open God's Word with confidence to inquire and to examine the Scriptures for yourself so you might indeed be set free.

It is my honor and privilege to open the Holy Scriptures with you. Let's get started!

Serving Him until I see Him,
Wendy

Session 1

Joseph

WAITING WELL STATEMENT

Waiting well teaches us to trust God's
ways rather than doubt His delays.

KEY VERSE

*Joseph's master took him and put him in prison, the
place where the king's prisoners were confined.*
Genesis 39:20

VIDEO LISTENING GUIDE

We can trust God's ways because His ways include His

Presence. The Lord was with Joseph (Genesis 39:20–21).

Protection. Joseph found favor with the guard (Genesis 39:21–22).

Provisions. Joseph was given charge over all that went on in prison, and everything he did was a success (Genesis 39:23).

~~_Outwait_~~ _Preparation_. The prisoners came to Joseph to interpret their dreams. This prepared him for a later assignment (Genesis 40:8).

Remember: God won't waste our wait, and neither should we.

ADDITIONAL NOTES

Our waiting is part of our preparation

waiting well teaches us to trust His ways

Rather than doubt his delays.

INTRODUCTION

We meet Joseph at the time of his birth in Genesis 30:23–24, "She became pregnant and gave birth to a son and said, 'God has taken away my disgrace.' She named him Joseph, and said, 'May the LORD add to me another son.'" The Bible is then silent about Joseph until his life story begins to unfold in Genesis 37.

Let's rewind to before Joseph's birth for a greater understanding of the animosity the older boys had for their younger brother. Long before any children entered the picture, the person who would become their father, Jacob, fell in love with Joseph's mother-to-be, Rachel. Jacob asked her father, Laban, for permission to marry her. Laban agreed, but on one condition: Jacob had to serve him for seven years. Jacob willingly got to work, and the seven years passed.

Sadly, Laban tricked Jacob by giving him Leah—Rachel's sister and the woman who would become mother to Joseph's older brothers. (I know … it sounds like a soap opera.) Jacob loved Rachel so much, he was willing to work for Laban another seven years to be married to her. Leah's sons surely could have sensed their father's great love for Rachel and his indifference toward their mother. All the details about Jacob's relationships with his wives and the births of his children (including Joseph) can be found in Genesis 29–30. We then meet Joseph again when he is seventeen.

WHEN GOD'S WAYS ARE HARD TO TRUST

Read Genesis 37:2–11. What specific reasons does Scripture give for the older brothers' hatred of Joseph? *Their fathers Love + his dreams of leading over his - family - Jealousy   God gave him talents*

Historical experts suggest that each of Jacob's sons would have owned a working man's coat. Solid in color. Shorter sleeves and shorter in length. Nothing more than a piece of cloth with a hole in the middle to slip over the person's head. We can imagine that Joseph's coat, however, was elaborate. The sewn-in sleeves would have hung down to his hands and the hem down to his ankles. Jacob's colorful and extravagant gift to Joseph sounded a clear message to his older sons: Joseph is my favorite, and I want everyone to know it.

Joseph set himself up for brotherly hostility by the way he behaved, but the brothers took their hostility to an incomprehensible level. God had a special plan for Joseph's life that He revealed through dreams. The exact interpretations of his dreams (that Joseph would be second-in-command of Egypt and save his family from famine) weren't communicated, but Joseph knew God. He knew God had given him the dreams. In his pride, he may have thought God would make these dreams come to pass sooner than later. And his brothers' actions must have taken the wind out of Joseph's sail.

Read Genesis 37:19–20 and Genesis 37:26–28. How could what happened to Joseph have caused him to not trust God's ways?

Circumstances Contradict what
his dreams told him.
abandonment -

It's unlikely that any of us have been thrown in a cistern and then sold to Midianite merchants. However, it is very likely that we have been mistreated in some way. How do you respond when you are wronged?

Process - Grieve - Anger - acceptance
then

youth -

When I've been done wrong, I've gotten angry at God for not sticking up for me and for not sticking it to the one who hurt me. The anger has turned to bitterness and poisoned my relationships with people and with the Lord.

If Joseph had any bitterness, he got rid of it. Long before the New Testament was written, Joseph demonstrated the truth of Ephesians 4:31–32, "Get rid of all bitterness, rage and anger, brawling and slander, along with every form of malice. Be kind and compassionate to one another, forgiving each other, just as in Christ God forgave you." Can I share a hard truth in love? God will not bless bitterness. The cost of holding on to pain is too high.

How does Genesis 39:2–3 demonstrate that Joseph had not allowed bitterness, rage, and anger to separate him from God?

He was granted success for Not
being bitter for his circumstances.

Not letting circumstances define
or change his true character!

Details of Joseph's relationship with God are not recorded in Scripture. However, the depth of his walk with God is implied. Unlike David, whose conversations with God are in his psalms, we don't have any documented dialogues between Joseph and God. Yet their intimate relationship is clear: "The LORD was with Joseph, so he succeeded in everything he did" (Genesis 39:2 NLT). This kind of intimacy develops through a personal relationship with and obedience to God. Joseph trusted God's ways, even though he had every reason to doubt His delays.

WHEN GOD'S WAYS ARE EASY TO DOUBT

One delay in God's plan can be difficult for us to navigate, yet it is doable if we maintain our closeness with Him. But what happens when we are sidetracked by yet another holdup? When a setback pops up, it becomes all too easy to doubt God and lose confidence in His plan.

Joseph, delayed once by jealous brothers, found himself waiting again on God's plan to come to fruition. While Joseph served Potiphar as his right-hand man, "Mrs. Potiphar" took a liking to the young, strong, handsome man. Joseph resisted the seductive woman over and over. But even though Joseph did the honorable thing, he was falsely accused and thrown into prison (Genesis 39:19–20). How could this be? How could God allow another interruption?

What if we paused in the pause to consider this: a delay might be a time to mature our faith and deepen our relationship with God. What if the delay is for our good?

That might be hard to hear. When I felt despair in my waits, that was not the encouragement I wanted. But there's hope. I wish to share with you a verse that will make all the difference in your wait. Write it. Highlight it. Underline it. Memorize it. Read Psalm 84:11.

*For the Lord God is the Sun + Sheild
The lord bestows favor + honor;
No good thing does he withhold
From those whom walk is
Blameless!*

Friend, God will not withhold anything good from you when you are walking with Him. But—yes, there is a _but_—we don't get to define *good*. We have to trust God to define good, even if good is a delay or a hardship. Perhaps Joseph had more lessons to learn. Maybe his pride needed to be humbled, leadership skills sharpened, or submission refined.

What are you waiting for in your life right now? How is God working during your current delay?

Some delays are longer than others and provide greater opportunities to learn to trust God. God provided Joseph with two years of trust training as he waited in the jail. Can you imagine spending two years being punished for something you didn't do? You may be able to relate to Joseph. Maybe you haven't been locked in a prison with bars, but maybe you have felt trapped in a prison of isolation, accusation, or contention. What do we do when serving an undeserved sentence?

Joseph spent his days in prison doing what he knew to do. He used the gift of his calling to help others. Instead of being mad at God, the dreamer interpreted dreams for other prisoners. This act did not go unnoticed. At just the right time, Pharaoh called on Joseph to interpret his dream. Joseph's waiting well and trusting God paid off.

Read Genesis 41:39–43. How did God reward Joseph for staying faithful to Him?

In charge of Pharaoh & Eygpt.
acknowledged his importance to
all of Eygpt.

List your gifts and how you can use them as you wait and trust in God's timing.

Pharaoh greatly expanded Joseph's territory and authority. This happened only because Joseph waited well. As far as Scripture reveals, he never questioned or rebelled against God. As Joseph served in Egypt, he had no idea that he was making a way to save his own family.

When a severe famine hit the land, his brothers left Canaan to purchase grain from Egypt's storehouses (Genesis 42). All of Joseph's training and trusting was put to the test when he came face to face with those who had betrayed him.

Read Genesis 45:4–15. How did Joseph respond to his disloyal brothers?

Compassion Even they did not deserve.

Think about a time when you were right even though others doubted you. When I'm right, my pride likes for others to know it—especially those who didn't believe me. Joseph's humble response challenges me. He demonstrated a great concern for God's righteousness and a total lack of concern for his own rightness.

Read Genesis 50:19–21. Joseph pointed to God's sovereign plan, and then he promised to provide for his brothers and their families. There wasn't any retaliation on his part for their sin against him. Joseph didn't gloat, "I told you so. You hurt me; now I will hurt you."

Think about it. When given the opportunity to point to God's righteousness or your rightness, which are you more likely to do, and why?

> As Faith + relationship with God grows better able to see God's Righteousness.

Even though we don't like them, delays are sometimes necessary. God never wastes one minute of our wait. He uses the pause to show us that His timing and ways are completely trustworthy. If we wait well, God will use the pause to prepare us for the moment our wait ends. Joseph stayed close to God through his twenty-year wait. When his wait ended, I have to think that God said, "Well done."

ON YOUR OWN ... IF YOU WANT TO

Read Galatians 5:22–23. As is stated in one of Chuck Swindoll's outlines on Joseph, "As a result of his circumstances, Joseph had only one freedom left—the freedom to choose his attitude."[1] When you are in the middle of a wait, what attitude do you choose?

Sometimes depends on situation but try not to

Which fruit of the Spirit do you need to ask God to give you more of and to help you receive as you wait?

Read Psalm 31:24. In an article on Joseph's faithfulness, Jon Bloom wrote, "Sometimes faithfulness to God and his word sets us on a course where circumstances get worse, not better. It is then that knowing God's promises and his ways are crucial. Faith in God's future grace for us is what sustains us in those desperate moments."[2]

Take a moment to consider past promises to you that God has been faithful to keep. Record them below.

1. God says he will always be there for us — Car accident cryiyout his Name + he protected me

2. Walked beside me through the tough times → times he carries us! losing my job - faith he would Provide / time to increase my faith

3. Protecting through bad decisions in my past (twenties)

[?] What are we holding on to that god/we wants us to throw down?

Session 2

Moses

WAITING WELL STATEMENT

Waiting well looks forward to the future
while staying present in the present.

KEY VERSE

staff
symbol of his ← *God has to do. Some*
authority *demonstrations to us!*

Then the LORD said to him, *"What is that in your hand?"*

"A staff," he replied.

Exodus 4:2

Exodus 3 - Burning Tree

VIDEO LISTENING GUIDE

What am I holding on to that may be holding me back from my future?

Maybe today is the day to throw down our

- bitterness and pick up the power of
  happiness.

- fear and pick up the power of
  Courage.

- unforgiveness and pick up the power of
  mercy.

- anger and pick up the power of

  <u> joy </u>.

- pride and pick up the power of

  <u> humility </u>.

- hostility and pick up the power of

  <u> Peace </u>.

• hate and pick up the power of
_____Love_____.

Remember: God won't waste our wait, and neither should we.

ADDITIONAL NOTES

INTRODUCTION

Moses's life and his contributions to biblical history are too vast to cover in one session. From his near-death experience as an infant (Exodus 1:15–2:10), to his murder of an Egyptian slave (Exodus 2:11–15), to the forty years he lived in Midian (Exodus 2:15–25), along with his face-offs with Pharaoh, the triumphant exodus from Egypt, and his exceptional leadership through the desert, Moses's life could (and does!) fill a book. Therefore, we will focus our study on the segment of his life in which he most effectively demonstrated this session's waiting well statement: his ongoing opposition to Pharaoh.

In general, waiting well is hard (I'm sure you're nodding your head in agreement), but waiting well in the face of constant opposition can seem downright impossible. God directly revealed Moses's future, and as soon as Moses reckoned with himself that he would obediently follow the Lord, opposition arose.

LOOKING FORWARD TO THE FUTURE

According to Exodus 3:16–18, what did Moses's future hold?

Gather elders of Israel
Bring you out of the
Lead them out of Egypt
& into Promise land

Looking forward to the future can be exciting, especially when we know the future holds some joyful event, like a wedding, the birth of a child, or a move to a new home. On the other hand, looking forward to the future has the potential to be intimidating when things are bleak or unclear. When that's the case, looking forward with hope, much less staying present in the present and working through our wait with God, is challenging.

Read Exodus 4:1, 10. Why did Moses feel apprehensive about the future plan God laid out before him?

Because he was not a good speaker

Currently, what future are you challenged to focus on?

Financial – Retirement
professional – work → Fear of do I change what is that?
health – physical
mental health
personal Relationship buldg w/ Howard + our future
Personal Relationship buldg w/ God

What misgivings about the future make you anxious as you attempt
to stay present in the present?

-finances
-Wedding preparation.
- Fear of the unknown
- Fear am I being tempted by Satan
  rather than hearing God !!!

Moses offered excuses to God, and so do I. Can you relate? My
heart is for God and His will, but often the assignment He gives me
appears to be beyond my current skill set. My faith takes a backseat
to fear. Like Moses, I sometimes wrestle with my doubts as I fight
to focus on my future. Fear forces our minds to oppose the truth we
know about God.

Ephesians 2:10 gives me confidence to drive away fear by remind-
ing me that my future is secure and has been perfectly planned since
the beginning of time. We just need to relax in the pause, stay present in the present, and embrace God's plan.

To help you experience this same confidence as you focus on the
future, write the words of Ephesians 2:10 in the space below. Then
read it aloud. You might be tempted to breeze past this part if you are
familiar with the verse. Oh, please, don't skip it! There is something
powerful and poignant about writing and reading God's Word.

Instead we are God's accomplishment
created in crist Jesus to do good things
God Planned for these good things to
be the way we live out lives!.

While we are waiting, God is preparing us for what He has already prepared for us. And since He has prepared a future for us, we can trust that He will not leave us to stumble and fumble our way through it. We are never alone in our waiting; God is always with us (Matthew 1:22–23), helping us resist the opposition. And He often allows a friend to come to our aid.

Oh, how I love my "God girls"!

Read Exodus 4:11–14. Who joined Moses and helped him stay focused on the future? *Aaron the Lavite of God*

In what ways has God helped you in your waiting?

Who is your "God girl" or "God guy"? What has she or he done to help you stay focused on the future?

Diana Robinson — positive /
Fred

(P)therapist (Sandy Springs) Christian Focus

God is not insensitive to the opposing forces of our fears and reservations about waiting well. He sees our potential and wants us to walk successfully into the future He has planned for us. Moses eventually found his leader legs and confidently overcame his fears, but not before he encountered further opposition—Pharaoh, king of Egypt.

We have an enemy who seeks to distract us from our future so we will not stay present in the present. Confidently trusting God as we look forward to the future is part of waiting well.

STAYING PRESENT IN THE PRESENT

Staying present in the present is where we experience God. In this place, He prepares us for the future He has prepared for us. The present is where we sense God's nearness, see His power, and are seasoned with His love. The present prepares us for our future. It's imperative we don't miss our present. Our enemy knows this, so he wreaks havoc around us.

We have a real enemy who desperately wants us to fail; his name is Satan (1 Peter 5:8–9). He seeks to divert our focus away from our future. He does this by using tactics that deter us from everything God wants to teach us as we stay present with Him in our wait.

It's vital we understand that we have an enemy who fights against us in the heavenly realms (Ephesians 6:12). But let's be real; we also have human enemies. They, like Satan, want to throw us off course so we will lose sight of our future and fail.

One definition on Dictionary.com describes an _enemy_ as "a person hostile or opposed to a policy, cause, person, or group, especially one who actively tries to do damage."[1]

Take a second to circle the word _actively_ in the definition above. One person actively opposed Moses's future, as well as the future of God's people. Pharaoh was Moses's enemy in the flesh. Every time Moses visited him with a warning from God, Pharaoh white-knuckled his grip on the Israelites and refused to release them, regardless of God's miraculous work through Moses's staff. How annoying! Moses finally submitted to God's plan and was faced with opposition at every turn. Let's see how Moses handled the diversion attempts.

Read Exodus 5:22; 6:12, 30; and 8:30 (you can split these verses up among your group). Who did Moses stay in constant contact with as his present was provoked with insecurities, doubts, and opposition?

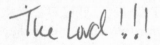
The Lord !!!

In Matthew 6:25–34, Jesus teaches about trusting God rather worrying about your tomorrows. We can certainly make application of His wise words to this session's waiting well statement. Jesus uses the word *seek* in verse 33. *Zéteó* is the Greek word for "seek," and it means "to seek out, search through, and to make a diligent search."[2]

Read Matthew 6:33. What does Jesus say will help us dispel all our concerns about our future?

God's Kingdom + God's Righteousness

What do you find most challenging about searching for and seeking out God, His kingdom, and righteousness?

Our enemy, who wants us to fail, is no match for our God, who wants us to succeed. Our future is too great to sacrifice by allowing ourselves to become sidetracked by opposition—whether earthly or from other realms. As we learn to stay present in the present, God will help us overcome our insecurities and strengthen us, despite our excuses. When we constantly turn to God, we and our faith will be well equipped to complete the good work He has prepared for our future.

ON YOUR OWN ... IF YOU WANT TO

Moses saw the power of God when he was willing to let go of his staff. For a shepherd, the staff represented power and protection. He used it as authority over the sheep, to guide them from one pasture to the other, and to rescue them from dangerous situations. It was his power.

Sometimes what we are holding on to can hold us back. Moses needed to see the power God could give if he would only trust Him. In this session's video, I mentioned some things we hold on to that could hold us back from truly experiencing God's power and movement toward the future He has planned for us.

In your prayer time this week, focus on one item each day. Courageously confront what God reveals about what you are holding tightly. Use the space provided to record your revelations.

- Let go of bitterness and pick up the power of happiness.

- Let go of fear and pick up the power of courage.

- Let go of unforgiveness and pick up the power mercy.

- Let go of anger and pick up the power of joy.

- Let go of pride and pick up the power of humility.

- Let go of hostility and pick up the power of peace.

- Let go of hate and pick up the power of love.

Session 3

David

[handwritten] Killed Goliath + Saul was not suppose to be King

WAITING WELL STATEMENT

Waiting well waits with God, not on God.

[handwritten] Rather than on God

KEY VERSE

[*But David thought to himself, "One of these days I will be destroyed by the hand of Saul. The best thing I can do is to escape to the land of the Philistines.]* Then Saul will give up searching for me anywhere in Israel, and I will slip out of his hand."

1 Samuel 27:1

[handwritten right margin] discourage ment caused him + makes a decision to flee to a tribe that is 100% against god.

[handwritten] Not give our thoughts the power! Feelings → Can lead us to discouragement

VIDEO LISTENING GUIDE

Waiting *on* God will give way to action based on human **reasoning**
and ~~thinking~~

39

When we wait *with* God, we make our decisions based on God's
reading.

Our feelings will lead us to

- places we shouldn't *go*.

  The giant-slaying hero chose to live among the Philistines in a town given to him by King Achish.

- seek the approval of people we wouldn't *normally associate with*

  David wanted to please Achish. David said to Achish, "If have found favor in your eyes" (1 Samuel 27:5). He sought approval from someone other than God.

- participate in things we would *never participate in*.

  David fought the Geshurites, Girzites, and Amalekites without direction from God. He went rogue in his raids and looting.

Remember: God won't waste our wait, and neither should we.

ADDITIONAL NOTES

INTRODUCTION

Let's look in on David nearly fourteen years after the prophet Samuel anointed him king.[1] David knew the truth: God appointed him to be king. Yet, over a decade after that promise had been given, another man still sat on the royal throne. A man who had tried over and over to kill David. The years of running from King Saul and fighting for his life had psychologically worn David down. The singer and his harp were silent. We have no record of any musical musings during this time in David's life. His stress had no outlet. David had hit rock bottom. The loudest voices he heard in his spiritual low were the thundering shouts of despair and discouragement.

We have all been there. Following hard after God, fully trusting Him for our future, but winding up falling lower than we ever imagined possible. *How did I end up here? When did I make the decision to cross that line? Where did it all go wrong?* The decline typically begins when we act on our own thoughts.

WAITING ON GOD

Waiting *on* rather than *with* God leads us to act on human reasoning. We see and hear and find information, then reason. We act on what we think we should do, based on our limited knowledge and our feelings, rather than wait for God's instructions.

Our thoughts can be dangerously destructive to the future God has planned. Scripture says, "But David thought to himself, 'One of these days I will be destroyed by the hand of Saul'" (1 Samuel 27:1a). Without a pause, his fear-filled thought gave way to human reasoning, "The best thing I can do is to escape to the land of the Philistines. Then Saul will give up searching for me anywhere in Israel, and I will slip out of his hand" (1 Samuel 27:1b). Oh, the places our thoughts and feelings will take us!

Where have your thoughts taken you when you felt certain there was no other way? *Negative + discouraged, empty fearful*

What sparked me when I was younger or Now

Our thoughts can take us to wrong places. But hallelujah, like my son says, "There's a verse for that." Read Philippians 4:8. How do we replace wrong thinking?

Finally brothers + sisters what ever is true noble, right, pure, lovely, admirable If any thing is excellent or praise worthy think about such things Think out the positives from the situation

Even though David knew what was right and true, he didn't have the emotional or mental strength to replace wrong thinking with right thinking. In his weakness, dark thoughts and fears silenced the truth. Destructive thinking doesn't happen overnight; it's a slow fade. In a moment of weakness, we allow one wrong thought to dictate our choice. As long as the result isn't too terribly disastrous, we continue to guide ourselves. We forget or deliberately choose not to seek God's leading or wise counsel from godly people. Then we find ourselves in a hornet's nest, making our own decisions—decisions that are based on self and do not honor God. David's slow fade began in 1 Samuel 21, when he began running from Saul, and continued in the wilderness of Maon (also called the Desert of Paran).

According to 1 Samuel 21:10, to where did David escape?

Akish King of Gath

Record David's actions 1 Samuel 25:39–44. What did he do upon hearing of Nabal's death? How many wives did David then have?

Praise be to the lord for his destruction

# of Wives – abaigale 2 Wives
         – aheninin 1 was given away
         – Michael Michael (sauls daughter) given away.

David's slippery slope was greased with constant stress, which set him on a course of bad decisions. He attempted to join the Philistines (remember Goliath?), and he broke God's marriage covenant. The emotional and mental weight of his circumstances was too much for him to bear and led him right back to the Philistine headquarters and King Achish.

Waiting is hard, but the slow fade is avoidable. To evade the fade, it's essential we take care of ourselves: mind, body, soul, and spirit. What things do you do to take care of these four parts of yourself?

Not enough! Yoga— Daily Devotions
Spirit —

Counselors and mental health experts can assist in improving our mental well-being. A commitment to physical exercise and healthy eating will support our physical fitness. Prayer, reading God's Word, and worship are the sources of wellness for our soul and spirit.

In black and white, these tips to flee the fade sound simple … but let's be real. In the dark moments of despair, we must reach deep within ourselves to think about that which is right, true, lovely, and praiseworthy. It takes strength to call a professional for help, to choose nourishing foods, and to set aside time in our busy schedule to be with God. In the moment, making healthy and God-honoring choices can feel overwhelming. But David found the strength and so can we.

When he fled Maon, after King Achish rejected him in 1 Samuel, David penned, "I will extol the LORD at all times; his praise will always be on my lips. I will glory in the LORD; let the afflicted hear and rejoice" (Psalm 34:1–2). When it is difficult to make the call, eat healthy, slow down, find words of praise—muster out with all the strength you have, "Help me, Lord."

Read Psalm 34:17–18. What does the Lord do when we cry out to Him? Who is the Lord near?

Righteous cry out —+ lord hears them + delivers them from all their troubles + Broken hearted is who the lord is near

It's imperative for us to tend to our total wellness. If we neglect the decline of our well-being, we are destined to repeat our sin and slide further away from God. The stakes are too high to ignore.

Read 2 Samuel 11:1–4, 14–17. Discuss David's decline. What led to the decisions he made? What were the results of those decisions—for David and for others?

*Bethsheba— Committed adultry
Bethsheba husband —out in front line + so he would die + he got killed
knowingly went against the 10 Comandments*

In no way am I suggesting that all discouragement leads to wrong thinking and is a precursor to sin, but it certainly played out that way in David's life. He followed his thoughts into the enemy camp and running to Nabal's territory to take Abigail as a bride, and back to enemy territory. Waiting on God can take us to places we never thought we'd go and convince us to do things we never dreamed we'd do. Waiting with God is such a better choice; it's the only choice.

WAITING WITH GOD

Waiting *with* God allows us to experience God while waiting on His instructions and refusing to reason with our thoughts alone. It recognizes His voice and finds peace in waiting and joy in obedience. There's no slow fade or slippery slope. There's only one path leading up and up, as obedience follows instruction.

Even when David was a young shepherd boy, his life was marked with a commitment to instruction as he faithfully obeyed his earthly father. This lifestyle cultivated a heart that pleased God, a heart that would one day lead God's beloved Israel. This is important to remember: obedience pleases God.

Select three people to read the following verses: Luke 11:28, Psalm 119:2, and Proverbs 16:20. What is God's response to obedience?

Luke 11:28 - God Blesses

19:2 - Blessings

16:20 - Blessings + prosperity

Although God surrounded David with the godly counsel of priests and military advisers, David still confidently approached God for instruction. In 1 Samuel 23, while on the run from Saul, David learned the Philistines had robbed the wheat-threshing floors in the town of Keilah. David wasn't king yet, but the men flocked to him with the report because they trusted him more than Saul. David didn't rush to battle; he asked for instruction.

Read 1 Samuel 23:1–5. In your own words, write what happened.

> Looking - Ask should we attack
> Go to Akela - he will give them the the
> Philistines
> Listened / asked for direction & then obeyed
> god / Did not let others influence his
> decisions.

The story gets better! David learned Saul was on his way to attack him. After such a big victory, pride could have welled up in David and caused him to hang around and fight Saul. But David inquired again of the Lord. Even after his triumph, David humbled himself to God's leadership (1 Samuel 23:9–14).

We can all agree obedience is important. But one question begs to be asked: How do we know if it is God giving instruction, or just our own heads reasoning out the situation? Since David is a shepherd, let's examine a sheep reference, just for fun.

Write John 10:14 in the space below.

I am th good sheperd & D Know my sheep + my sheep know me!

The sheep recognize the shepherd's voice because they spend time together. When my best friend calls me, her picture shows up on my phone's screen. I think that's so cool! But even if her picture didn't appear, when I answered, would I know it was her calling? Of course I would! I recognize her voice because I spend time with her.

We will only be certain of God's instruction when we recognize God's voice. We will only recognize God's voice when we spend time with Him. Each day our schedule needs to include some time with God that is centered on His Word and prayer.

Think about your schedule for the coming week. When can you find time to spend with God?

*Jesus Calling — Sarah Young
God Calling —*

When we put the right stuff in, the right stuff will come out. Before long, our natural response to despair and discouragement will be positive encouragement as well as the overwhelming desire to seek God for the next step. It's in the seeking and obeying that we experience God. This makes waiting with Him become second nature, not to mention a complete joy.

According to Jeremiah 29:13, what will we find when we seek God?

Find God - When we seek him

ON YOUR OWN ... IF YOU WANT TO

In Psalm 139:23–24, David invites God to investigate his life. Challenge yourself with this prayer, and record what God reveals. I love Eugene Peterson's paraphrase of this verse (from *The Message*):

> Investigate my life, O God, find out everything about me; cross-examine and test me, get a clear picture of what I'm about; see for yourself whether I've done anything wrong—then guide me on the road to eternal life.

One definition of the word *investigate* says that it means "to search out and examine the particulars of in an attempt to learn the facts about something hidden, unique, or complex."[2] I'll admit, this prayer didn't come easy for me. I was sold out on the idea of God examining my heart and revealing anything I was doing wrong; however, praying this prayer for a year changed my life ... well, God did.

How do you feel about inviting God to investigate your life?

What is God revealing as you pray?

Are you willing to align with what He reveals in His Word?

waitig withGod Not
for god.

God wants us to Experience God while we are waiting on [?] with him

Session 4

Nehemiah

WAITING WELL STATEMENT

**Waiting well is more about experiencing
God rather than enduring the delay.**

KEY VERSE *Cupbarrie - taste the cup before the King*

*If it pleases the king and if your servant has found favor
in his sight, let him send me to the city in Judah where
my ancestors are buried so that I can rebuild it.*

Nehemiah 2:5

VIDEO LISTENING GUIDE

Progressive perseverance means ___Steady___ ___Continuous___ movement with a purpose. *(slow + steady get*

53

Progressive perseverance starts with ___*prayer*___. Nehemiah's prayer consisted of confession of sin, praise, and begging for favor. Prayer is our communication to the heart of God.

Progressive perseverance faces ___*insults*___ and ___*oppositions*___ but doesn't lose focus on God. Sanballat, Tobiah, and Geshem, regional governors for the king of Persia, took every advantage of the opportunity to sabotage the work of God's people. We have an enemy who tries to sabotage our wait journey. When God presses pause, Satan applies the pressure.

Progressive perseverance holds on to ___*word of God*___. Nehemiah reported that neither he nor his men put down their weapons. As they made progress, they held a tool in one hand and a weapon in the other. Scripture is our weapon of warfare against our enemy. *" Really put our knees to the Good News("*

Progressive perseverance knows prayer ___*continues*___. Peppered throughout the wall-building drama, you will find Nehemiah on his knees. After ugly words and taunts, the prophet stops to pray. We have to begin the wait in prayer, continue in prayer, and end in prayer.

Remember: God won't waste our wait, and neither should we.

ADDITIONAL NOTES

Progressive

Start our waiting prayer.

INTRODUCTION

A few lessons ago, we studied Moses and the impact Satan desires to make on our future. He is the enemy to all God wants to accomplish in our lives. Even though we can't see Satan, he is real and confronts us with opposition. I know—it doesn't seem fair, particularly when we are trying to wait well but are overwhelmed with all manner of opposition.

Grab on to this hope and tuck it deep in your heart: if the opposition to God's work in our lives is excessive, then what God is trying to accomplish must be extravagant.

In this session, we are going to expound on the teaching points from the video. The points are too valuable and the text is too rich to gloss over. God wanted to accomplish something extravagant through Nehemiah, and his enemies knew it. His response to these antagonists will equip us to endure our delay victoriously, while also having the immense pleasure of experiencing God.

EXPERIENCE GOD: PRAY ABOUT IT

We're all guilty of drive-by prayer. You know, those one-line, half-hearted mumblings. Okay … (insert ho-hum sigh and slight eye roll) I'll pray about it. So, we pray, but without really wanting to get to the heart of the matter, only wanting God to fix it. I'm guilty of doing this. But Nehemiah was not. He took prayer seriously.

Even though King Cyrus of Persia had released the captives to return to Jerusalem to rebuild the city, it was still in shambles. The wall-less city lay vulnerable to attack, and the people weren't safe.

This news brought Nehemiah to his knees. He loved Jerusalem and longed to help repair the city and its people.

Nehemiah was a man of action—patient action. He didn't pack a wagon with shovels and supplies, hire a team of builders, or gather his posse and storm off to Jerusalem. Instead, he "sat down and wept. For some days, [he] mourned and fasted and prayed before the God of heaven" (Nehemiah 1:4).

Please underline the words *some days* in the verse above. In preparation to meet with King Artaxerxes to ask for a leave of absence from his cupbearer position, Nehemiah committed to diligent prayer. Four months would go by before he spoke to the king about his request. Since Nehemiah was still mourning at that time (Nehemiah 2:1–3), we can assume that he continued to pray and think about Jerusalem during those four months.

How long do you typically pray about something before you take action?

Depends on the situation

Read Nehemiah 1:5–11. Let's pull this scripture apart and let Nehemiah teach us how to pray.

- Praise God (v. 5b).

    God is worthy of our praise, thanks, and
    worship. Every day we wake up, we have an
    opportunity to see God working and to be in
    His presence. We can honor Him with praise,
    not just for what He does, but for who He is to
    us in the midst of our wait.

- Ask God to listen (vv. 6a, 11).

    Sounds kind of silly, doesn't it? I mean, isn't
    God already listening? Asking for help doesn't
    imply He isn't listening; it humbles us before
    the only One who can truly help. We have
    become so self-sufficient, we have forgotten the
    All-Sufficient One.

- Confess to God (vv. 6b–7).

    This is not a blanket forgive-me-of-all-my-sins request, and then we move on. I'll admit: I like blanket prayers like this, especially when confessing my sin. Sin is ugly, and I don't want to see my ugliness in the light of God's holiness. However, Nehemiah got down to specifics when he prayed, "We have acted very wickedly toward you. We have not obeyed the commands, decrees and laws you gave your servant Moses." As difficult as it might be, we need to take time to be real about our sin and confess it to the Lord.

- Remind God of His Word (vv. 8–9).

    Nehemiah reminded God of His covenant with His people. Reminding God of His Word isn't implying He's forgotten what He said. Recalling God's promises helps us remember His faithfulness. The reminding is more for us than for God.

Nehemiah prayed *and* fasted. A friend recently said, "If you want to put some power in your prayer, fast." I didn't believe her, and I wasn't going to fast (with crossed arms and lips pursed), until I found myself in the position of not waiting well. The wait was becoming increasingly frustrating. One day, as I cried out to God, my friend's words echoed in my mind.

The following Monday, I began to fast. Fasting gives us the opportunity to take our eyes off the things of this world to focus on God. We sacrifice food, television, social media—we put aside our selfish nature so we can hear God more clearly and know Him more intimately. The movement He does on our behalf as a result of our fasting is icing on the cake.

How does your prayer life resemble or differ from Nehemiah's example?

Praying and fasting work, girls. Nehemiah and the Israelites completed the wall around Jerusalem in fifty-two days! A fifty-two-day project with a four-month foundation of prayer. Wow ... simply wow!

EXPERIENCE GOD: PERSEVERE

We've established that waiting is hard. The degree of difficulty is amped up to another level when opposition rises up to criticize what you are doing. Whether you are parenting a wayward child, working to make ends meet, or praying over your calling—you may feel like you are barely hanging on. However, you are partnering with God. As you work hard to cooperate with God while He works, you don't need the added pressure of insults and mockery.

Read Nehemiah 4:1–3. Have you ever heard such words? How did you respond? *Feeble jews*

Insults / criticizing

Sadly, the world is full of mean people who prove the old adage wrong: Sticks and stones may break my bones, and words *will* hurt me. My natural response to insults and attacks is to sharpen my claws and fight back. What about you? What is your instinctive reaction to criticism?

Nehemiah's response to his bullies teaches us that we don't have to fall prey to or push back against our attackers. Read Nehemiah 4:4–5, 8–9. What did Nehemiah do in response to his attackers?

Let God Handle the Confrontation
Prayed — to response to attackers.

Each time the mean kids on the playground taunted Nehemiah, he tattled on them. Yes, adult tattletaling (sort of). Our fellow waiter took his frustrations to God. Someone else we know prayed for those who insulted Him. Turn to Luke 23:34 to find out who.

Jesus endured the greatest betrayal, pain, and insults known to mankind. Yet, in the midst of it all, He prayed for those who were hurting Him. Jesus persevered through His assignment; so did Nehemiah. Let us follow their examples, and obey Paul's advice when he said to "bless those who persecute you; bless and do not curse" (Romans 12:14). Continued prayer—prayer without ceasing (1 Thessalonians 5:17)—helps us persevere through the insults and our wait to experience God, rather than just endure the delay.

EXPERIENCE GOD: HOLD ON TO HIS WORD

Prayer certainly helps us stay on the offense during our wait and supports our defense when others try to insert themselves into God's work in our lives. But there are times when we must pull out the heavy artillery to defend our position with greater fervor.

Nehemiah continued to report the rude behavior of Sanballat and Tobiah, neighboring governors and resident troublemakers, to God. But then they took their assault beyond a war with words. They launched a physical attack. Some people will not be able to handle your successful and growing relationship with God; they just won't. These men didn't like the Israelites' success and pulled out all the stops to try to cause them to fail.

The people were tired and afraid, just like you and I can get when we try to wait well. Read Nehemiah 4:14. What did Nehemiah tell the people? Don't be afraid of the ~~believe in Jesus~~ who Fights for us! Fight for

Read Nehemiah 4:18. What did the builder wear on his side as he worked? Swords

Nehemiah told the people to remember that the Lord was on their side and to carry their weapons at all times. In most cultures today, it's not acceptable or legal to carry a sword on your hip, much less wield it against an enemy. However, there is a sword we can carry and use to defend ourselves from those who are trying to disrupt our waiting well.

Read Ephesians 6:17. What is the sword of the Spirit?

Gods Words

Friends, when we hold on to God's Word, it will hold on to us. As we read, study, and live out what the Bible says, it becomes part of who we are. The power of Scripture becomes our strength. Even if we don't have actual Bibles in our hands, the words we study and live are ingrained in our thinking. When we can call out the Word of God, the enemy will flee.

"But what if I can't remember it word for word? What if I mix up a reference?" Live in the liberty of God's grace. The Word of God is powerful but doesn't suddenly become powerless because you can't recall it verbatim or you forget a reference. It will accomplish what it is intended to accomplish. For example, James 4:7 says, "Submit yourselves, then, to God. Resist the devil, and he will flee from you." Satan has to flee when we resist him and submit to God.

There's power in the Word, but we can't use the Word as a weapon if we don't know it. Take time to read, study, and memorize the Word. It is our most powerful weapon against our enemy.

I want to do more than just endure the delays in my wait. I long to experience God and to embrace every opportunity to know Him better. Don't you? Nehemiah's lessons on waiting well have equipped us with the tools necessary to do the same and to get to know God while He works on our behalf.

ON YOUR OWN ... IF YOU WANT TO

Author and speaker Nancy DeMoss Wolgemuth said this about Nehemiah:

> At every turn, Nehemiah's intuitive response was to lift his eyes to heaven and seek wisdom and help from above. He knew that the task to which he was called was far bigger than himself, and that he could not possibly succeed without divine intervention and enabling.[1]

What are you waiting on right now? Write out a prayer to God, following Nehemiah's example.

- Praise God.

- Ask God to listen.

- Confess to God.

- Remind God of His Word.

Session 5

Abraham and Sarah

WAITING WELL STATEMENT

> Waiting well focuses on the Person of our
> faith rather than the object of our wait.

KEY VERSE

*Then the word of the LORD came to him: "This man will not be your
heir, but a son who is your own flesh and blood will be your heir."*

Genesis 15:4

VIDEO LISTENING GUIDE

We know we've lost sight of the Person of our faith when we

70

- _____ _____ to an alternative idea (Genesis 16:1–2).

- _____ to an alternative idea (Genesis 16:2a).

- _____ to an alternative idea (Genesis 16:3–4).

If we do lose sight of the Person of our faith, we can be confident that our _____ does not mess up _____ (Genesis 17:15–16).

Remember: God won't waste our wait, and neither should we.

ADDITIONAL NOTES

INTRODUCTION

This session's waiting well statement is by far the most challenging for me. It exposes a great weakness: my wants. When I have a want, I want it yesterday. Maybe you can relate.

Sarai knew what it was to wait. Her name was Sarai before God changed it to Sarah (Genesis 17:15), and she had been waiting for a baby all her life. Abram, her husband, whose name was changed to Abraham (v. 5), wanted an heir. It's important to note the significance of their name changes. God had promised Abram that he would be the father of many nations and, therefore, gave him a name that meant "father of many." And Sarai would be called Sarah, meaning "princess to many." Yet even though they had received the promise and had the names to prove it, they were still unable to conceive. But God knew the desires of their hearts, and would fulfill their desires, in His time.

That's the part about waiting that trips me up: "in His time."

Our world tells us we don't have to wait. We have instant messaging, instant mail, instant meals, and instant merchandising. With this kind of influence, it's easy to see how waiting can create unrest in our spirit. The unrest causes us to lose our focus on the Person of our faith.

OUR WANT: THE OBJECT OF OUR WAIT

Why should I keep my eyes on the Person of my faith when it seems like He has forgotten me? Welcome to my thoughts from 1994 to 1996, when month after month, the display on the pregnancy test was a minus rather than a plus. I've walked in Sarai's sandals. I wanted a baby, and having one became an obsession. In my rising, standing, and sleeping, being pregnant was all I ever thought about. I know how it feels to want to quit on God.

Identify the object of your wait. If you desire, share with the group.

Before we throw God and His promises out the window because we don't have the object of our wait, let's truly examine what we want. Write Psalm 37:4. What are your thoughts about this verse?

The promise isn't meant as a guarantee that we will get everything we want: "God's gonna give me the desires of my heart. Yeah. I love God, and I'd like a new job." The psalmist uses the word *delight* when describing our relationship with God. The root of the Hebrew word for *delight* that is used here means "to be soft or pliable." When our hearts are soft and pliable, we are able to bend to God's will. We can get to know God through time spent in His Word and in prayer. In getting to know God we experience the pleasure of being in His company, and have the overwhelming desire to delight in Him.

In what do you delight?

Something supernatural happens in the delighting process. One day, we realize God's deep love for us. We long for the things He longs for, and want what He wants.

I never asked God if it was His desire for me to conceive a child. I wanted to have a baby. Period. The end. But as I started living and delighting in the Lord, things began to change.

After two years of doing all I could to get pregnant, I finally threw my hands up and said, "God, it's in Your hands. If You want me to have a baby, I will. If You don't, I won't. I accept Your plan. Help me delight in You and Your ways." My desire had to be surrendered to His desire. I needed to recognize that He was enough and that I could be satisfied in Him, with or without a child.

Read Genesis 15:1–5. Who was having a conversation with Abram? What promise was made and by whom?

Abram delighted in God's ways. This conversation is evidence of the intimate relationship he and God shared, and God knew Abram's heart was to do His will.

God knows you. Oh, how He longs for you to know Him, experience His great love for you, and be completely fulfilled, with or without the object of your wait. The Person of our faith is enough. This is where we have to land in our wait because there is no other way to have peace in our pause.

What's keeping you from a deep, intimate relationship with God? Is it fear? anger? unbelief? Write about it here.

OUR FOCUS: THE PERSON OF OUR FAITH

Delighting in the Lord doesn't suddenly make us happy about waiting. I didn't rejoice that I was still childless and throw baby showers for my friends who were living my dream. The desire to have a baby was still real, but I made the decision to trust God's timing and plan. In the waiting and delighting, the Person of my faith became someone I wanted to know. Here's what I found out about who He is.

He is believable.

Read Genesis 15:6. How did Abram respond to what God told him?

A man in his seventies was told that he would have offspring as numerous as the stars in the sky, and he believed. The scripture doesn't say he believed *in* God. "Abram believed the LORD, and he credited it to him as righteousness" (Genesis 15:6). Abram believed God. When it comes right down to it, we must decide whether or not we believe God.

In my various seasons of wait, I tiptoed through the waters of really believing God. *Is He who He says He is? Can He do what He says He can do?* With fear and trembling I dove into daring to believe by living His truth.

When I didn't want to give, I gave. Guess what? It *is* more blessed to give than to receive (Acts 20:35). An overflow of blessings *does* flow when I tithe (Malachi 3:10). In being still I *can* know that He is God (Psalm 46:10). Obedience *is* better than sacrifice (1 Samuel 15:22).

Believing God is how we make it through the tough times and can truly celebrate in the moments we experience Him.

What do you find most difficult about believing God?

Oh, friend, cast your doubt aside and dare to believe! He is believable. And He is trustworthy.

He is trustworthy.

Yes. God will do what He says He will do. "Then the word of the LORD came to him: 'This man will not be your heir, but a son who is your own flesh and blood will be your heir'" (Genesis 15:4). Even though Abram and Sarai tried to make God's promise come to pass by their methods (16:1–4), God kept His word. He did what He said He would do.

What happened in Genesis 21:1–2?

No matter how much meddling we do, we can't mess up God's plan. Our manipulation might extend our wait while God works through the troubles that our interference has caused (see Genesis 16 and what happened with Abram, Sarai, and Hagar), but God's plan will prevail. And it is a good plan, worthy of our wait. His plan is good, and so is He.

He is good.

In our lowest times of waiting, sometimes it's hard to believe God is good. Yeah, I said it. *If God is good, then why hasn't my child returned home? If God is good, then why am I still single? If God is good, then why do I still have college debt looming over my head?* Oh, I wish I could open the Bible and help you know the answers to your questions, and mine. I don't know why, but this I do know—God is good. If He wasn't good, you and I would be facing eternity apart from Him.

You may know this verse, but turn to John 3:16. What did God do to show His goodness and love for you?

If God was good enough to send His only Son to save us, who did nothing to deserve saving, isn't He good enough to trust through the wait? Doesn't this kind of sacrifice—this selfless love—prove that He's good enough to believe?

Through my years of waiting I've been mad at God, manipulated situations, and done the exact opposite of what I knew He wanted me to do, yet He continued to be faithful to me. I'm so unworthy of this life I live.

But when we wait well, and our wait ends, we will discover that the object of our wait pales in comparison to the Person of our faith. This is truth. Underline it. Highlight it. Write today's date in the margin, because when your wait ends, you can come back to this page and write "YES!!!" The wait is a reward, because in the wait we get to know God in a way we wouldn't know Him if we never had to wait.

Don't rush the wait.

ON YOUR OWN ... IF YOU WANT TO

The Person of our faith is believable, trustworthy, and good. These truths are hard to hold on to while we wait. The enemy shouts all the things that are going wrong, and tries to silence what is good about God. Spend some time with God reflecting on these questions.

How is God demonstrating His believability to you?

> And my God will meet all your needs according to the riches of his glory in Christ Jesus. (Philippians 4:19)

How is God demonstrating that He is trustworthy?

The one who calls you is faithful, and he will do it.
(1 Thessalonians 5:24)

How is God good to you?

The LORD is good, a refuge in times of trouble. He cares for those who trust in him. (Nahum 1:7)

Worship our good God by singing "God Is So Good."

Session 6

Noah *[handwritten: pattern of obedience]*

WAITING WELL STATEMENT

> Waiting well pushes through the pause
> by doing what we know to do.

KEY VERSE

[handwritten: Command - direct us / specific authority]
[handwritten: everything - Every single thing]

Noah did everything just as God commanded him.

Genesis 6:22

VIDEO LISTENING GUIDE

Sometimes our wait comes

- because of someone else's
  <u>decisions</u>.

"The LORD saw how great the wickedness of the human race had become on the earth, and that every inclination of the thoughts of the human heart was only evil all the time" (Genesis 6:5).

- as a source of ____*discipline*____.

"So the LORD said, 'I will wipe from the face of the earth the human race'" (Genesis 6:7).

- to purify our ____*faith*____.

No matter how we arrive at our wait, our response to our wait is to do what we know to do—to obey God. We find Noah's response in one verse: "Noah did everything just as God commanded him" (Genesis 6:22).

Command means "to direct with __Command__ ."

Everything means "__Every Single thing__ ."

Remember: God won't waste our wait, and neither should we.

ADDITIONAL NOTES

INTRODUCTION

Maybe if we added all the years we've been waiting on God; the total would equal the years this man waited. At the tender age of four hundred and something, Noah was approached by God concerning a building project. The world God created was corrupt and a huge disappointment, so He decided to start over. God told Noah to build an ark, that rain was coming, and that He was going to wipe away everything except Noah's family and some animals. I feel sure Noah wasn't aware that he was making a 120-year-long "yes" to God.

I have the attention span of a goldfish. When my waiting takes longer than a week or so, I'm ready to jump in with both feet and help God out. My family would have been washed away in the flood if the ark-building project had been assigned to me. Not Noah. He waited well and persevered by doing what he knew to do. We can learn a lot about pushing through the pause by examining the character of Noah.

PUSHING THROUGH THE PAUSE

How is Noah described in Genesis 6:9?

Righteous Blameless Faithful

No wonder Noah could continue doing what he knew to do; he was righteous and blameless. This is the thought that raced through my mind when I first read this scripture. *Righteous* and *blameless* are big Bible words that are hard to digest. They are intimidating and can make us feel ill equipped for the wait, as well as unworthy of God's love. Let's liberate ourselves with a vocabulary lesson.

Righteous is translated as "just"; it is the Hebrew word *tsaddiq* (tsad·dēk').[1] The word means "guided by truth, reason, justice, and fairness."[2] Our second word, *blameless,* gives a little more insight into Noah's character. This word is also translated as "perfect" (as if *blameless* isn't daunting enough). Before we all roll our eyes and say "Impossible," we have to remember the only person who has ever lived a perfect life is Jesus Christ. (Insert deep sigh of relief.) The Hebrew word for *perfect* in this verse is *tamim* (taw-meem'), and it means "having integrity, innocent, wholesome." The words "without sin" are nowhere to be found in the definition. I feel so much better, don't you?

Noah was a good guy, a law-abiding citizen who lived by truth and was full of integrity when dealing with people. Genesis 6:9 concludes with "and he walked faithfully with God." In short, he hung out with God and lived a life God could trust. You know what? This seems doable!

What do you find most challenging about being a good girl, living by truth, and being full of integrity in dealing with people?

What does Genesis 6:22, 7:5, 7:9, and 7:16 say about Noah?

Did Everything -   obedient
Did All the Lord Commanded.
Man & Woman came to Noah
Man & Female Animals

Noah obeyed the Lord. There is so much to be said about the
importance and the power of obedience. I've never been one who
liked to be told what to do. In this session's video, I referred to
myself as a "bossy pants." Over time I've learned "obedient pants"
fit much nicer. I'll admit, it took awhile for me to embrace an
obedient way of life.

The things God asks us to do can sometimes seem off the
wall, and are often counter culture (like building an ark when
there's no rain), but there is freedom in the words "Yes, Sir." God
is so much fun! His ways are not our ways, and His thoughts are
not our thoughts: He can be quite creative. We get to be part of
secret acts of kindness to someone who needs a helping hand.
He invites us into conversations with people who just need to
be noticed. And, on occasion, about the time you need a lesson
in humility, maybe the bathroom at your hair salon needs to be
cleaned—twice.

Read John 14:15. What are we demonstrating to God when we obey?

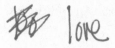 love

Noah did everything God commanded him to do. God was very specific and His directions were very clear. Noah walked with God; therefore, God knew He could trust Noah with the job and Noah would be faithful to push through a long wait to complete the task.

How do you feel about obeying everything God asks you to do?

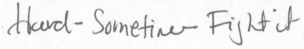 Hard - Sometime - Fight it

There was so much sin and idolatry in the world during the time of Noah's wait. I can only imagine the ridicule he and his family had to endure as, day in and day out, they showed up at the job site. "Hey, Noah, what is that you're building? A what? An ark? Because God is gonna send rain? Right. Hey, Noah, what is rain?"

There will be people around who won't understand what you're going through. "Why are you waiting? You should move forward. God is silent because you're just sitting there. God helps those who help themselves." Friends, don't give in to the false narrative of unwise counsel. Surround yourself with people who are likeminded—people who are walking with God, living by truth, and demonstrating integrity.

Read Isaiah 40:29–31. How does our faithful God help us remain faithful to Him as we continue to do what we know to do?

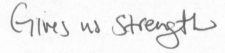

Gives us Strength

DOING WHAT YOU KNOW TO DO

What do Christians know to do? If I asked this question in a room of twenty-five people, I'd probably get twenty-five different answers with one central theme: be like Christ. We won't be perfect—only Jesus was perfect—but we can work hard to reflect Christ to a world who desperately needs Him.

What do Romans 12:1 and Ephesians 5:1–2 teach us about imitating Christ?

*offer Body as a loing sacrifice)
Follow Gods example*

Go Back to the living Sacrifice

Jesus demonstrated His love for the world by sacrificing His life. I'm not suggesting it is necessary for you to climb onto a cross or become a martyr for the faith. Being a living sacrifice means giving our lives completely over to God and His teachings. God wants us to set ourselves apart from the world so the world will see Him through us. Christ was in this world, but separated from it by His actions.

Jesus didn't avoid the lepers; He touched them. He didn't condemn the woman caught in adultery; He showed her compassion. When He encountered hungry people, He fed them. He helped the sick and reached out to the outcast.

Jesus loved people—all people. He gave Himself up for people. This is how the world will know Christ and His love.

Write John 13:35 in the space below.

By this everyone will know that you are my disciples if you love one another.

While we wait, why not love others? Spend time helping those in need. Check with your local food pantry, homeless shelter, crisis pregnancy center, and church. Someone is in need today. People will know we belong to God when we demonstrate sacrificial love like Jesus did; then they will want to know Jesus too. When we wait well by doing what we know to do, whether it's building an ark or taking food to a shut-in, the objects of our wait become less important, and we can push through the pause.

King David, while on the run from his enemies, cried out to God, "My times are in your hands" (Psalm 31:15). This is the best way to surrender the angst and anxiety of our wait.

Indeed, Lord, our times are in Your hands.

ON YOUR OWN ... IF YOU WANT TO

In Philippians 1:6, Paul encourages those who are waiting, "being confident of this, that he who began a good work in you will carry it on to completion until the day of Christ Jesus." I love the truths in this verse! He first gladdens our heart with a reminder that the work God is doing is good, then reassures us of God's faithfulness to complete it.

What do you find most difficult about pushing through the pause?

While you are pushing through the pause, what efforts can you make to help others?

Often our pause is more palatable when we look away from the object of our wait to lift up another person. Call your church office to see how you can get involved. It may mean helping a clothes-closet ministry, organizing a food drive, or visiting and praying for shut-ins.

Write Isaiah 64:4 in the space below. Underline the words *no one.*

What an amazing way to end our study! God will do something in our lives that no eye has seen, no ear has heard, and no mind can conceive *if* we wait (also translated as "hope") in Him. Oh, wait well, my dear friend! Open your eyes, ears, and mind. God is doing something incredible in your life. I don't want you to miss it.

The Portrait Gallery

Do you love pictures? I do! My home and office are filled with photos. At any moment I can glance at them, and I'm able to relive my children's history, from infancy to graduation. The stories of my precious family members are preserved in frames. One of my favorite pictures is of my grandmother. She went to be with Jesus a few months shy of her ninety-ninth birthday. This particular black-and-white image is special because she is beautiful, healthy, and happy. Her smile fills her face as she stands on the front porch with her hair and apron blowing in the breeze. Oh, the story it tells!

Wouldn't it be fun to see pictures of the people we've studied? Not watercolor illustrations that hang on church walls or felt caricatures from Sunday school, but real photographs. Until we are gathered around the throne of God and walk the streets of the new

Jerusalem, we have only our imaginations and biblical knowledge to create images of them in our minds. So, let's do that together!

The "Portrait Gallery" will help you get to know our fellow waiters from Scripture. You will learn all sorts of information and fun facts about each person: Where are they from? How do they connect with other parts of the Bible? What is their family history? At the conclusion of your walk in the gallery, you will have enough knowledge to fill your mind with an array of portraits of your family—these brothers and sisters in the Lord.

About Joseph

PERIOD

Scholars debate when Joseph lived. Some suggest he was born about the middle of the 1500s BC.[1] However, we do know from the biblical account that he lived 110 years, through one of Egypt's terrible famines. *Joseph* means "Jehovah will add."

PLACES IN SCRIPTURE

Joseph is mentioned in both the Old Testament and the New Testament (Acts 7:9–18; Hebrews 11:21–22). His life story is recorded in Genesis 37–50.

PERSONAL BACKGROUND

Joseph was the eleventh son of Jacob, and the firstborn son of Rachel. Rachel was Jacob's beloved wife. His special affection for her poured over into a special love for Joseph. Out of this fond affection, Jacob treated his youngest son better than his other boys. Joseph worked hard as a shepherd, like his brothers, but he also reported (upon Jacob's request) to his father the habits of his brothers. While the other ten sons had regular coats, at the age of seventeen, Joseph received a special coat of many colors from his father. This infuriated the brothers. To add fuel to their fire, Joseph shared dreams with them that indicated his family would one day bow down to him. The brothers' jealousy overcame their judgment, and they plotted to kill Joseph.

Judah reasoned with his brothers to sell Joseph to Ishmaelite slave traders rather than to kill him. The brothers agreed. They covered up their evil deed by telling their father that a wild animal had killed Joseph, even offering him Joseph's bloodstained and ripped coat as proof.

Joseph didn't deserve to be sold into slavery. He traveled a long way from home to palaces—and to prisons. Through it all, God knew exactly where Joseph was, even if Jacob and his brothers did not. God used Joseph's trials to raise him (in Chuck Swindoll's words) "from the pit of slavery to the pinnacle of power."[2] No one knew the brothers' actions had set Joseph on a path to fulfill the God-given dreams and eventually save their entire family.

It would be easy to admire Joseph's godly character and praise God's sovereignty yet miss the silent, desperate years of pain Joseph endured. He could have seethed with anger and set his sights on revenge, but he chose to trust God's ways rather than doubt God's delays.

PERSPECTIVE AND APPLICATION

Often, our wait throws us into a pit. Like Joseph, we can trust God, even if it seems our faithfulness to God and His Word has set us on a course where circumstances get worse, not better. No matter how dismal our current circumstances may seem, God's story will not be circumvented. At the end of our wait, we can say that what others intended for harm, God used for our good (Genesis 50:20).

About Moses

PERIOD

Moses was born about four hundred years after Joseph's rule, during the time when the Egyptians had enslaved the Hebrews. At the time of Moses's birth, Pharaoh had issued a decree to kill all Hebrew baby boys.

PLACES IN SCRIPTURE

Moses's life story begins in the book of Exodus and ends in Deuteronomy. Moses is mentioned almost eighty times in the New Testament; Hebrews and Acts tell the most about him.

PERSONAL BACKGROUND

It is rare to have the privilege to study a person's life from birth to death. We meet Moses in Exodus 2. His life can be divided into three forty-year sections.

Birth to age 40: Moses was born to Amram and Jochebed, of the tribe of Levi. He lived with his parents and his siblings, Miriam and Aaron, in Egypt. Moses's parents hid him from Pharaoh's deadly decree as long as they could, then Jochebed devised a plan that saved her son's life. She placed him in a waterproof basket and put him in the grasses of the Nile River. Pharaoh's daughter found and rescued Moses, and raised him as her own son. He grew up in the royal palace and had the best of everything.

Despite his noble nurturing, Moses stayed keenly aware of his Hebraic roots. His compassion for and kinship with the Jews led him to murder out of anger an Egyptian slave master who had been mistreating a Hebrew slave. In fear of Pharaoh's punishment, Moses fled to Midian.

Ages 40 to 80: In the pastures of Midian, Moses met and married Zipporah. He worked for his father-in-law, Jethro, a Midianite priest. God used this time in Moses's life to prepare him to be a loving father and protective shepherd. Moses was tending sheep in the wilderness on Horeb, the mountain of God, when God spoke to him through the burning bush. The message shook the shy and unconfident man to his core. God's message was, "I have surely seen the affliction of my people who are in Egypt and have

heard their cry.... Come, I will send you to Pharaoh that you may
bring my people, the children of Israel, out of Egypt" (Exodus
3:7, 10 ESV).

Ages 80 to 120: Moses obeyed God and returned to Egypt. He
convinced the Hebrews to prepare to leave Egypt. God graciously
allowed Moses's brother, Aaron, to help convey God's message of the
Israelites' freedom to Pharaoh. Yet Pharaoh refused to release God's
people. God used Moses, Moses's staff, and Aaron as He produced
plagues that rained calamities on the Egyptians. After ten plagues,
Pharaoh finally released the Israelites.

Moses faithfully led God's people through the desert. God
faithfully provided for and protected His people. Moses was the
mediator of the old covenant (part of God's promises to Abraham
and his descendants) and gave the people the Mosaic law—the Ten
Commandments and over six hundred individual commands with
detailed instruction on how God was to be worshipped and how
the people should live (Exodus 19–24).[3]

God did not allow Moses to enter the Promised Land because
of his disobedience at the waters of Meribah Kadesh (Numbers
20:12; Deuteronomy 32:51). He brought the Israelites to the
borders of Canaan, but he did not go in.[4] Moses died at 120 years
of age.

PERSPECTIVE AND APPLICATION

Moses stayed present in the present to hear God and experience
God's power working in his life. He pushed through his doubts

and fears to faithfully walk toward the future of being the Israelites' leader. His commitment to God never wavered, even when his wait did not end as he had expected. Whether our wait ends as expected or unexpectedly, God remains faithful—and we should remain faithful too.

About David

PERIOD

David lived seventy years and reigned as King of Israel for forty years, around 1010–970 BC.

PLACES IN SCRIPTURE

David is anointed king in 1 Samuel 16. His life and tenure as king runs through 2 Samuel 12. He is the author of seventy-six psalms and is also mentioned in 1 Chronicles. The New Testament references David in Acts 13:22, Matthew 1:17, and Luke 1:31–33.

PERSONAL BACKGROUND

We meet David as a young teenager tending his father's flock of sheep in the pasture. God sent the prophet Samuel to David's home to offer a sacrifice with his family and to anoint Israel's next king. The prophet reviewed Jesse's presented sons, but God did not affirm any of them to take the throne. Instead, God confirmed—and Samuel anointed—David, the unlikely son, as king. With no further instructions, the prophet returned to Ramah, and David returned to the pasture.

Over time, David began working at the palace as a harp player for King Saul. When he wasn't soothing Saul with his musical talent, David tended his father's sheep on the slopes of Bethlehem's pastures. As noted by John MacArthur, "Doubtless, David learned important lessons regarding the weight of responsibility during this time, lessons that were later put to use in ruling over Israel"[5]

David made his public debut during a toe-to-toe battle with the Philistine giant Goliath. Upon bringing his soldier-brothers provisions on the battlefield, David heard the giant taunting the Israelites and the Lord. David stepped up as the only man brave enough to face Goliath. In defense of the Lord's name and the Israelite army, David slayed the giant with his shepherd's tools. Killing lions and bears as he'd protected his flock had trained David well for that moment.

King Saul promoted David from musician to his armor-bearer and a commander of a thousand. Saul made David part of his family when he gave his daughter's hand in marriage to David. But David's closeness to Saul only fueled the king's envy and hatred toward his son-in-law and soon-to-be successor. Because of this, David spent much of his wait on the run from Saul.

This shepherd-turned-solider had to bide his time in hard places before Saul died and David could rightfully take his place as king. These hardships, along with others later in his life, led him to pen many of the psalms. In them, we see that David learned the importance of waiting with God, not just waiting on God.

Shortly after Saul's death, David and his allies took control of Judah. Though he conquered Jerusalem several years later, he was forced to wait before being declared king over all of Israel. During this time, David married three more wives and subsequently had many children (perhaps the most well known being Solomon).

Even though David was a man after God's own heart, he sinned. Israel's king had an affair with another man's wife and later had her husband murdered on the front lines of battle. God forgave David's sin, but he had to live with the sin's consequences. Deceit, backstabbing, rape, and murder entangled his family. His sons revolted against him and conspired to overthrow his kingship.

PERSPECTIVE AND APPLICATION

When the wait goes long, our patience runs short. Discouragement and doubt can take root in our hearts if we don't see God's activity on our behalf. In these long seasons, our feelings will lie and tell us to "make things happen" or "God is not gonna come through for you." David struggled with similar fears and frustrations.

Instead of rehearsing these pains, retreat to the pleasure of God's plan. It's always best to wait with God and experience His power rather than wait on God and try to make things happen on our own.

About Nehemiah

PERIOD

The exact date of Nehemiah's birth is not known. It is thought that he was born in the fifth century BC while the Israelites were under Babylonian captivity.

PLACES IN SCRIPTURE

The book of Ezra mentions Nehemiah. Though the book of Nehemiah bears his name and much of it is written as a first-person account, Nehemiah did not write it. No one knows for certain who the author is, though many believe that Ezra, his contemporary, penned it.

PERSONAL BACKGROUND

Nehemiah's father was Hakaliah, from the line of Judah, and he had one brother, Hanani. As a youth, Nehemiah served as cupbearer and trusted consultant to the Persian ruler King Artaxerxes I. At that time, the Persians had gained political control from the Babylonians. The Hebrews had returned to Jerusalem following their seventy years of exile in Babylon. Sadly, the city was in shambles. The city walls laid in ruin, leaving its inhabitants vulnerable to enemy attacks.

Nehemiah had a deep love for his homeland and his people. The knowledge of the state of affairs saddened him: "When I heard these things, I sat down and wept. For some days I mourned and fasted and prayed before the God of heaven" (Nehemiah 1:4). After this time with God, Nehemiah determined to lead a third wave of Jewish exiles back to Jerusalem. As Norman Geisler noted, "Nehemiah's expertise in the king's court equipped him adequately for the political and physical reconstruction necessary for the remnant to survive."[6] God had providentially placed Nehemiah in a position of leadership and in good standing with the king; therefore, Nehemiah confidently approached the king for help. The king granted Nehemiah permission to return to Jerusalem to assist in the rebuilding of the city walls. Once Nehemiah arrived in Jerusalem, he exchanged his title of cupbearer for governor.

Nehemiah became the target of opposition and accusations. He chose not to turn against his enemies, but instead turned to his Lord. We bear witness to Nehemiah's strength through the time he spent in prayer, seeking wisdom on how to lead the people and rebuild. We are fortunate to have front-row seats to Nehemiah's commitment to his people and the rebuilding, as he demonstrated how waiting well is not just enduring God's delays but experiencing Him as we wait.

God moved in the hearts of the Israelites to help Nehemiah's mission. They donated so much money, goods, and labor that the wall was rebuilt in fifty-two days! After the completion of the wall, Nehemiah and Ezra gathered the people and read to them the book of the Law. This served as a reminder that God was their true fortress and protector.

PERSPECTIVE AND APPLICATION

Nehemiah spent time waiting on the Lord, and he reaped the benefits of experiencing God's presence and favor. The key to Nehemiah's successful wait was his intentional prayer life. What an incredible challenge his life offers to all of us waiters! In order to experience God, rather than just endure His delays, we have to be purposed to pray. It is through prayer we gain the fortitude to wait well, and in the waiting and the praying, we experience God.

About Abraham and Sarah

PERIOD

Abraham was born under the name Abram, in the city of Ur in Babylonia. Some scholars suggest that he was born around 1800 BC. Sarah was Abraham's half-sister, the daughter of his father but not of his mother.[7] Sarah was born Sarai and raised in the Ur of the Chaldees, which was located in what is now southern Iraq.

PLACES IN SCRIPTURE

Abraham's story begins in Genesis 11, and his death is recorded in Genesis 26. Sarah is first mentioned as Abraham's wife in Genesis 11. Abraham is listed in Jesus's genealogy in Matthew 1:1 and again in

Romans 4. The Hall of Faith in Hebrews 11:8–12 gives both Abraham and Sarah honorable mentions.

PERSONAL BACKGROUND

Abram (renamed Abraham in Genesis 17) is seventy-five years old when we first meet him in Scripture. He lived with his father, Terah, an idol merchant, and two brothers, Nahor and Haran, in Ur of the Chaldeans. Very little is recorded about his early life.

He moved from Ur to Haran (the land) with his father, his wife, Sarai (later renamed Sarah), and his nephew, Lot. After Abram's father died, God told Abram to move to Canaan. This call to move was accompanied by an enormous covenantal promise: "I will make you into a great nation, and I will bless you; I will make your name great, and you will be a blessing" (Genesis 12:2). Dr. Keith H. Essex, an associate professor of Bible exposition, summarized the covenant in this way: "The elements of the covenant are threefold: making Abraham into a great nation, blessing Abraham personally, and blessing all nations in Abraham. The promises of the covenant are unconditional. The rest of the OT repeatedly refers back to God's oath to Abraham in the Torah. The NT does the same by pointing out that Jesus Christ, Abraham's seed, will make possible the final fulfillment of that covenant in the future."[8]

God reaffirms His covenant with Abraham in Genesis 15:4–6, saying, "A son who is your own flesh and blood will be your heir." Then God brought him outside and said, "Look up at the sky and count the stars—if indeed you can count them … So shall your offspring be." Scripture tells us that Abram "believed the LORD, and he credited it to him as righteousness."

Despite these powerful promises, Abram and Sarai gave in numerous times to their doubts and fears that they would never conceive. Sarai gave Abram her maidservant, Hagar, who became pregnant with Abram's first son, Ishmael. Thirteen years later, the Lord spoke again of His promises to Abram and renamed him *Abraham*, meaning "father of many nations" (Genesis 17:4). God also renamed Sarai, *Sarah*, meaning "princess" and (as noted by John MacArthur) "the ancestress of the promised nations and kings."[9]

Even though Abraham and Sarah tried to manipulate God's plan, God fulfilled His promise with the birth of Isaac. Because of their advanced ages, there could be no doubt that this baby was a gift and miracle from God.

Abraham was tested when God asked him to sacrifice this miracle. (Isaac was twenty years old at the time.) His response demonstrated that he completely trusted the Person of his faith and was no longer focused on the object of his wait. With the knife raised above his head, Abraham heard the voice of the angel of the Lord, "Do not lay a hand on the boy.... Now I know that you fear God, because you have not withheld from me your son, your only son" (Genesis 22:12). As one author summed up this story, "The point is that Abraham's faith in God was greater than his love for his son, and he trusted that even if he sacrificed Isaac, God was able to bring him back from the dead (Hebrews 11:17–19)."[10]

Sarah lived to be 127 years old, and Abraham to 175. Before his passing, he found a wife for his son Isaac from his brother's family. We see God's promises to Abraham fulfilled through Isaac's offspring.

PERSPECTIVE AND APPLICATION

Manipulation to "help" God's plan come to fruition is not the answer. Waiting is never wasting time. As we stay focused on the Person of our faith, peace will fill our spirit and enable us to wait well. Abraham and Sarah temporarily took their eyes off God, but their mistake did not mess up God's plan. God's grace was applied, and His plan prevailed. What awesome comfort to anyone who messes in God's business more than they should!

About Noah

PERIOD

Noah was born in the tenth generation from Adam. He is thought to have lived around 2704–1755 BC. He died at the age of 950.

PLACES IN SCRIPTURE

Noah's story begins in Genesis 5 and concludes in chapter 9. He is mentioned three times in the New Testament: 1 Peter 3:20, 2 Peter 2:5, and Hebrews 11:7, in the Hall of Faith.

PERSONAL BACKGROUND

Noah was the son of Lamech. He was married and had three sons, Shem, Ham, and Japheth. He lived in a time of increasing sinfulness and wickedness on the earth. Noah and his family were the only humans deemed righteous in the whole world. Noah walked with God. God told Noah of His plans for the world: "I am going to put an end to all people, for the earth is filled with violence because of them" (Genesis 6:13). But God gave Noah instructions about how He intended to spare Noah and his family during the flood: "So make yourself an ark of cypress wood.... I am going to bring floodwaters on the earth to destroy all life under the heavens, every creature that has the breath of life in it. Everything on earth will perish. But I will establish my covenant with you, and you will enter the ark—you and your sons and your wife and your sons' wives with you" (vv. 14–18). The account continues with more instructions for Noah, and then we are told, "Noah did everything just as God commanded him" (v. 22).

Noah faithfully obeyed the Lord. For 120 years, he pushed through the pause by doing what he knew to do. He spent those years building the ark to the exact blueprints and specifications the Lord had given him. True to His word, when the ark was completed, the Lord sent the rain and flooded the earth.

Noah pushed through another pause. He and his family rode out the storm for over a year in the ark, under God's protection. When Noah, his family, and all the creatures departed from the ark, he built an altar to the Lord and offered a burnt offering. Pleased with Noah's sacrifice, God said, "Never again will I curse the ground because of humans, even though every inclination of the human heart is evil from childhood. And never again will I destroy all living creatures, as I have done" (Genesis 8:21).

God then sealed this promise with a covenant to Noah: "I have set my rainbow in the clouds and it will be the sign of the covenant between me and the earth.... Whenever the rainbow appears in the clouds, I will see it and remember the everlasting covenant between God and all living creatures of every kind on the earth" (Genesis 9:13–16).

PERSPECTIVE AND APPLICATION

Noah endured two long pauses in his life by doing what he knew to do: obeying God. Obedience is paramount to navigating paths of our wait. God will lead us and give instructions. It is up to us to follow the leading and obey His orders, even if He asks us to build an ark.

Notes

SESSION 1: JOSEPH

1. Charles R. Swindoll, "Joseph: A Man of Integrity and Forgiveness," Message Mate series, 1980, 2015, www.insightforliving.org.uk/broadcast/jos-0, accessed August 21, 2017.

2. Jon Bloom, "Joseph: Staying Faithful When Things Just Get Worse," DesiringGod.org, March 1, 2010, www.desiringgod.org/articles/joseph-staying-faithful-when-things-just-get-worse.

SESSION 2: MOSES

1. Dictionary.com, s.v. "enemy," www.dictionary.com/browse/enemy?s=t, accessed June 1, 2017.

2. *Strong's Exhaustive Concordance of the Bible*, s.v. "*zéteó*," Bible Hub, http://biblehub.com/greek/2212.htm, accessed June 1, 2017.

SESSION 3: DAVID

1. "Timeline: 1 Samuel," Bible Hub, http://biblehub.com/timeline/1_samuel/1.htm, accessed June 1, 2017.

2. Dictionary.com, s.v. "investigate," www.dictionary.com/browse/investigate?s=t, accessed June 1, 2017.

SESSION 4: NEHEMIAH

1. Nancy DeMoss Wolgemuth, "The Wall Is Broken Down," *Revive Our Hearts*, www.reviveourhearts.com/articles/the-wall-is-broken-down/, accessed June 1, 2017.

SESSION 6: NOAH

1. *Strong's Exhaustive Concordance of the Bible*, s.v. "*tsaddiq*," Bible Hub, http://biblehub.com/hebrew/6662.htm, accessed June 1, 2017.

2. Dictionary.com, s.v. "just," www.dictionary.com/browse/just?s=t, accessed June 1, 2017.

THE PORTRAIT GALLERY

1. Information about the dates of the lives of the Bible people mentioned in this study can be found in multiple scholarly sources, and it's difficult to pinpoint even approximate times with absolute certainty. For the purposes of this study, we have relied on information from the Jewish Virtual Library (www.jewishvirtuallibrary.org).

2. Charles R. Swindoll, "Joseph: A Man of Integrity and Forgiveness," Message Mate series, 1980, 2015, www.insightforliving.org.uk/broadcast/jos-0, accessed August 21, 2017.

3. "What Was the Purpose of Levitical Law?," GotQuestions.org, www.gotquestions.org/Levitical-Law.html, accessed June 1, 2017.

4. "Why Are the Circumstances of the Death of Moses So Mysterious?," GotQuestions.org, www.gotquestions.org/death-of-moses.html, accessed June 1, 2017.

5. John MacArthur, *The MacArthur Study Bible* (Nashville: Thomas Nelson, 1997), 400.

6. Norman L. Geisler, *A Popular Survey of the Old Testament* (Peabody, MA: Prince, 2007), 165.

7. "Sarah," Jewish Virtual Library, www.jewishvirtuallibrary.org/sarah-2, accessed June 1, 2017.

8. Keith H. Essex, "The Abrahamic Covenant," *The Master's Seminary Journal*, 10/2 (Fall 1999), 191–212, www.tms.edu/m/tmsj10n.pdf.

9. MacArthur, *MacArthur Study Bible*, 40.

10. "What Can We Learn from the Life of Abraham?," GotQuestions.org, www.gotquestions.org/life-Abraham.html, accessed June 1, 2017.

Waiting Well with God

In the *Wait and See Bible Study Kit*, Wendy Pope shows us how popular biblical figures did, or didn't, wait well as they found their places in God's plans. This kit is ideal for a women's small group to build community while learning how to wait well together. Designed for busy women, the study requires no outside homework or additional reading.

Contact a David C Cook rep at 800.323.7543
or visit your local Christian bookstore